COPYRIGHT © 2018 AUNT MEG AND ME JOURNALS™
ALL RIGHTS RESERVED.

NAME AND RELATIONSHIP TO PARENTS

_____

_____

ADVICE FOR PARENTS

_____

_____

_____

WISHES FOR BABY

_____

_____

_____

GUESTS

NAME AND RELATIONSHIP TO PARENTS

_____

_____

ADVICE FOR PARENTS

_____

_____

_____

WISHES FOR BABY

_____

_____

_____

GUESTS

NAME AND RELATIONSHIP TO PARENTS

_____

_____

ADVICE FOR PARENTS

_____

_____

_____

WISHES FOR BABY

_____

_____

_____

NAME AND RELATIONSHIP TO PARENTS

_____

_____

ADVICE FOR PARENTS

_____

_____

WISHES FOR BABY

_____

_____

_____

GUESTS

NAME AND RELATIONSHIP TO PARENTS

_____

_____

ADVICE FOR PARENTS

_____

_____

_____

WISHES FOR BABY

_____

_____

_____

NAME AND RELATIONSHIP TO PARENTS

_____

_____

ADVICE FOR PARENTS

_____

_____

WISHES FOR BABY

_____

_____

_____

GUESTS

NAME AND RELATIONSHIP TO PARENTS

_____

_____

ADVICE FOR PARENTS

_____

_____

_____

WISHES FOR BABY

_____

_____

_____

NAME AND RELATIONSHIP TO PARENTS

_____

_____

ADVICE FOR PARENTS

_____

_____

_____

WISHES FOR BABY

_____

_____

_____

GUESTS

NAME AND RELATIONSHIP TO PARENTS

_____

_____

ADVICE FOR PARENTS

_____

_____

_____

WISHES FOR BABY

_____

_____

_____

NAME AND RELATIONSHIP TO PARENTS

_____

_____

ADVICE FOR PARENTS

_____

_____

WISHES FOR BABY

_____

_____

_____

GUESTS

NAME AND RELATIONSHIP TO PARENTS

_____

_____

ADVICE FOR PARENTS

_____

_____

_____

WISHES FOR BABY

_____

_____

_____

NAME AND RELATIONSHIP TO PARENTS

_____

_____

ADVICE FOR PARENTS

_____

_____

WISHES FOR BABY

_____

_____

_____

GUESTS

NAME AND RELATIONSHIP TO PARENTS

_____

_____

ADVICE FOR PARENTS

_____

_____

_____

WISHES FOR BABY

_____

_____

_____

GUESTS

NAME AND RELATIONSHIP TO PARENTS

_____

_____

ADVICE FOR PARENTS

_____

_____

WISHES FOR BABY

_____

_____

_____

GUESTS

NAME AND RELATIONSHIP TO PARENTS

_____

_____

ADVICE FOR PARENTS

_____

_____

_____

WISHES FOR BABY

_____

_____

_____

GUESTS

NAME AND RELATIONSHIP TO PARENTS

_____

_____

ADVICE FOR PARENTS

_____

_____

_____

WISHES FOR BABY

_____

_____

_____

GUESTS

NAME AND RELATIONSHIP TO PARENTS

_____

_____

ADVICE FOR PARENTS

_____

_____

_____

WISHES FOR BABY

_____

_____

_____

GUESTS

NAME AND RELATIONSHIP TO PARENTS

_____

_____

ADVICE FOR PARENTS

_____

_____

_____

WISHES FOR BABY

_____

_____

_____

GUESTS

NAME AND RELATIONSHIP TO PARENTS

_____

_____

ADVICE FOR PARENTS

_____

_____

_____

WISHES FOR BABY

_____

_____

_____

NAME AND RELATIONSHIP TO PARENTS

_____

_____

ADVICE FOR PARENTS

_____

_____

WISHES FOR BABY

_____

_____

_____

NAME AND RELATIONSHIP TO PARENTS

_____

_____

ADVICE FOR PARENTS

_____

_____

WISHES FOR BABY

_____

_____

_____

GUESTS

NAME AND RELATIONSHIP TO PARENTS

_____

_____

ADVICE FOR PARENTS

_____

_____

_____

WISHES FOR BABY

_____

_____

_____

GUESTS

NAME AND RELATIONSHIP TO PARENTS

_____

_____

ADVICE FOR PARENTS

_____

_____

_____

WISHES FOR BABY

_____

_____

_____

NAME AND RELATIONSHIP TO PARENTS

_____

_____

ADVICE FOR PARENTS

_____

_____

_____

WISHES FOR BABY

_____

_____

_____

GUESTS

NAME AND RELATIONSHIP TO PARENTS

_____

_____

ADVICE FOR PARENTS

_____

_____

_____

WISHES FOR BABY

_____

_____

_____

GUESTS

NAME AND RELATIONSHIP TO PARENTS

_____

_____

ADVICE FOR PARENTS

_____

_____

_____

WISHES FOR BABY

_____

_____

_____

NAME AND RELATIONSHIP TO PARENTS

_____

_____

ADVICE FOR PARENTS

_____

_____

_____

WISHES FOR BABY

_____

_____

_____

GUESTS

NAME AND RELATIONSHIP TO PARENTS

_____

_____

ADVICE FOR PARENTS

_____

_____

_____

WISHES FOR BABY

_____

_____

_____

NAME AND RELATIONSHIP TO PARENTS

_____

_____

ADVICE FOR PARENTS

_____

_____

_____

WISHES FOR BABY

_____

_____

_____

GUESTS

NAME AND RELATIONSHIP TO PARENTS

_____

_____

ADVICE FOR PARENTS

_____

_____

_____

WISHES FOR BABY

_____

_____

_____

GUESTS

NAME AND RELATIONSHIP TO PARENTS

_____

_____

ADVICE FOR PARENTS

_____

_____

_____

WISHES FOR BABY

_____

_____

_____

GUESTS

NAME AND RELATIONSHIP TO PARENTS

_____

_____

ADVICE FOR PARENTS

_____

_____

_____

WISHES FOR BABY

_____

_____

_____

NAME AND RELATIONSHIP TO PARENTS

_____

_____

ADVICE FOR PARENTS

_____

_____

_____

WISHES FOR BABY

_____

_____

_____

GUESTS

NAME AND RELATIONSHIP TO PARENTS

_____

_____

ADVICE FOR PARENTS

_____

_____

_____

WISHES FOR BABY

_____

_____

_____

GUESTS

NAME AND RELATIONSHIP TO PARENTS

_____

_____

ADVICE FOR PARENTS

_____

_____

_____

WISHES FOR BABY

_____

_____

_____

GUESTS

NAME AND RELATIONSHIP TO PARENTS

_____

_____

ADVICE FOR PARENTS

_____

_____

_____

WISHES FOR BABY

_____

_____

_____

GUESTS

NAME AND RELATIONSHIP TO PARENTS

_____

_____

ADVICE FOR PARENTS

_____

_____

_____

WISHES FOR BABY

_____

_____

_____

GUESTS

NAME AND RELATIONSHIP TO PARENTS

_____

_____

ADVICE FOR PARENTS

_____

_____

_____

WISHES FOR BABY

_____

_____

_____

GUESTS

NAME AND RELATIONSHIP TO PARENTS

_____

_____

ADVICE FOR PARENTS

_____

_____

_____

WISHES FOR BABY

_____

_____

_____

GUESTS

NAME AND RELATIONSHIP TO PARENTS

_____

_____

ADVICE FOR PARENTS

_____

_____

_____

WISHES FOR BABY

_____

_____

_____

GUESTS

NAME AND RELATIONSHIP TO PARENTS

_____

_____

ADVICE FOR PARENTS

_____

_____

_____

WISHES FOR BABY

_____

_____

_____

NAME AND RELATIONSHIP TO PARENTS

_____

_____

ADVICE FOR PARENTS

_____

_____

WISHES FOR BABY

_____

_____

GUESTS

NAME AND RELATIONSHIP TO PARENTS

_____

_____

ADVICE FOR PARENTS

_____

_____

_____

WISHES FOR BABY

_____

_____

_____

GUESTS

NAME AND RELATIONSHIP TO PARENTS

_____

_____

ADVICE FOR PARENTS

_____

_____

_____

WISHES FOR BABY

_____

_____

_____

GUESTS

NAME AND RELATIONSHIP TO PARENTS

_____

_____

ADVICE FOR PARENTS

_____

_____

_____

WISHES FOR BABY

_____

_____

_____

NAME AND RELATIONSHIP TO PARENTS

_____

_____

ADVICE FOR PARENTS

_____

_____

_____

WISHES FOR BABY

_____

_____

_____

GUESTS

NAME AND RELATIONSHIP TO PARENTS

_____

_____

ADVICE FOR PARENTS

_____

_____

_____

WISHES FOR BABY

_____

_____

_____

GUESTS

NAME AND RELATIONSHIP TO PARENTS

_____

_____

ADVICE FOR PARENTS

_____

_____

_____

WISHES FOR BABY

_____

_____

_____

GUESTS

NAME AND RELATIONSHIP TO PARENTS

_____

_____

ADVICE FOR PARENTS

_____

_____

_____

WISHES FOR BABY

_____

_____

_____

GUESTS

NAME AND RELATIONSHIP TO PARENTS

_____

_____

ADVICE FOR PARENTS

_____

_____

_____

WISHES FOR BABY

_____

_____

_____

GUESTS

NAME AND RELATIONSHIP TO PARENTS

_____

_____

ADVICE FOR PARENTS

_____

_____

_____

WISHES FOR BABY

_____

_____

_____

NAME AND RELATIONSHIP TO PARENTS

_____

_____

ADVICE FOR PARENTS

_____

_____

WISHES FOR BABY

_____

_____

_____

GUESTS

NAME AND RELATIONSHIP TO PARENTS

_____

_____

ADVICE FOR PARENTS

_____

_____

_____

WISHES FOR BABY

_____

_____

_____

NAME AND RELATIONSHIP TO PARENTS

ADVICE FOR PARENTS

WISHES FOR BABY

NAME AND RELATIONSHIP TO PARENTS

_____

_____

ADVICE FOR PARENTS

_____

_____

_____

WISHES FOR BABY

_____

_____

_____

NAME AND RELATIONSHIP TO PARENTS

_____

_____

ADVICE FOR PARENTS

_____

_____

_____

WISHES FOR BABY

_____

_____

_____

GUESTS

NAME AND RELATIONSHIP TO PARENTS

_____

_____

ADVICE FOR PARENTS

_____

_____

_____

WISHES FOR BABY

_____

_____

_____

NAME AND RELATIONSHIP TO PARENTS

_____

_____

ADVICE FOR PARENTS

_____

_____

_____

WISHES FOR BABY

_____

_____

_____

GUESTS

NAME AND RELATIONSHIP TO PARENTS

_____

_____

ADVICE FOR PARENTS

_____

_____

_____

WISHES FOR BABY

_____

_____

_____

NAME AND RELATIONSHIP TO PARENTS

_____

_____

ADVICE FOR PARENTS

_____

_____

WISHES FOR BABY

_____

_____

_____

NAME AND RELATIONSHIP TO PARENTS

_____

_____

ADVICE FOR PARENTS

_____

_____

_____

WISHES FOR BABY

_____

_____

_____

GUESTS

NAME AND RELATIONSHIP TO PARENTS

_____

_____

ADVICE FOR PARENTS

_____

_____

_____

WISHES FOR BABY

_____

_____

_____

GUESTS

NAME AND RELATIONSHIP TO PARENTS

_____

_____

ADVICE FOR PARENTS

_____

_____

_____

WISHES FOR BABY

_____

_____

_____

GUESTS

NAME AND RELATIONSHIP TO PARENTS

_____

_____

ADVICE FOR PARENTS

_____

_____

_____

WISHES FOR BABY

_____

_____

_____

GUESTS

NAME AND RELATIONSHIP TO PARENTS

_____

_____

ADVICE FOR PARENTS

_____

_____

_____

WISHES FOR BABY

_____

_____

_____

NAME AND RELATIONSHIP TO PARENTS

_____

_____

ADVICE FOR PARENTS

_____

_____

_____

WISHES FOR BABY

_____

_____

_____

NAME AND RELATIONSHIP TO PARENTS

_____

_____

ADVICE FOR PARENTS

_____

_____

_____

WISHES FOR BABY

_____

_____

_____

GUESTS

NAME AND RELATIONSHIP TO PARENTS

_____

_____

ADVICE FOR PARENTS

_____

_____

_____

WISHES FOR BABY

_____

_____

_____

GUESTS

NAME AND RELATIONSHIP TO PARENTS

_____

_____

ADVICE FOR PARENTS

_____

_____

_____

WISHES FOR BABY

_____

_____

_____

GUESTS

NAME AND RELATIONSHIP TO PARENTS

_____

_____

ADVICE FOR PARENTS

_____

_____

WISHES FOR BABY

_____

_____

NAME AND RELATIONSHIP TO PARENTS

_____

_____

ADVICE FOR PARENTS

_____

_____

_____

WISHES FOR BABY

_____

_____

_____

GUESTS

NAME AND RELATIONSHIP TO PARENTS

_____

_____

ADVICE FOR PARENTS

_____

_____

_____

WISHES FOR BABY

_____

_____

_____

GUESTS

NAME AND RELATIONSHIP TO PARENTS

_____

_____

ADVICE FOR PARENTS

_____

_____

_____

WISHES FOR BABY

_____

_____

_____

GUESTS

NAME AND RELATIONSHIP TO PARENTS

_____

_____

ADVICE FOR PARENTS

_____

_____

WISHES FOR BABY

_____

_____

_____

GUESTS

NAME AND RELATIONSHIP TO PARENTS

_____

_____

ADVICE FOR PARENTS

_____

_____

_____

WISHES FOR BABY

_____

_____

_____

GUESTS

NAME AND RELATIONSHIP TO PARENTS

_____

_____

ADVICE FOR PARENTS

_____

_____

_____

WISHES FOR BABY

_____

_____

_____

GUESTS

NAME AND RELATIONSHIP TO PARENTS

_____

_____

ADVICE FOR PARENTS

_____

_____

_____

WISHES FOR BABY

_____

_____

_____

GUESTS

NAME AND RELATIONSHIP TO PARENTS

_____

_____

ADVICE FOR PARENTS

_____

_____

_____

WISHES FOR BABY

_____

_____

_____

GUESTS

NAME AND RELATIONSHIP TO PARENTS

_____

_____

ADVICE FOR PARENTS

_____

_____

_____

WISHES FOR BABY

_____

_____

_____

GUESTS

NAME AND RELATIONSHIP TO PARENTS

_____

_____

ADVICE FOR PARENTS

_____

_____

WISHES FOR BABY

_____

_____

_____

GUESTS

NAME AND RELATIONSHIP TO PARENTS

_____

_____

ADVICE FOR PARENTS

_____

_____

_____

WISHES FOR BABY

_____

_____

_____

GUESTS

NAME AND RELATIONSHIP TO PARENTS

_____

_____

ADVICE FOR PARENTS

_____

_____

_____

WISHES FOR BABY

_____

_____

_____

NAME AND RELATIONSHIP TO PARENTS

_____

_____

ADVICE FOR PARENTS

_____

_____

_____

WISHES FOR BABY

_____

_____

_____

GUESTS

NAME AND RELATIONSHIP TO PARENTS

_____

_____

ADVICE FOR PARENTS

_____

_____

_____

WISHES FOR BABY

_____

_____

_____

NAME AND RELATIONSHIP TO PARENTS

_____

_____

ADVICE FOR PARENTS

_____

_____

_____

WISHES FOR BABY

_____

_____

_____

NAME AND RELATIONSHIP TO PARENTS

_____

_____

ADVICE FOR PARENTS

_____

_____

_____

WISHES FOR BABY

_____

_____

_____

GIFT RECEIVED   GIVEN BY

_____   _____

_____   _____

_____   _____

_____   _____

_____   _____

_____   _____

_____   _____

_____   _____

_____   _____

_____   _____

_____   _____

GIFT RECEIVED   GIVEN BY

_____   _____

_____   _____

_____   _____

_____   _____

_____   _____

_____   _____

_____   _____

_____   _____

_____   _____

_____   _____

GIFT RECEIVED	GIVEN BY

GIFT RECEIVED	GIVEN BY
_____	_____
_____	_____
_____	_____
_____	_____
_____	_____
_____	_____
_____	_____
_____	_____
_____	_____
_____	_____

GIFT RECEIVED	GIVEN BY
_____	_____
_____	_____
_____	_____
_____	_____
_____	_____
_____	_____
_____	_____
_____	_____
_____	_____
_____	_____
_____	_____

GIFT RECEIVED	GIVEN BY

GIFT RECEIVED   GIVEN BY

_____   _____

_____   _____

_____   _____

_____   _____

_____   _____

_____   _____

_____   _____

_____   _____

_____   _____

_____   _____

_____   _____

GIFT RECEIVED	GIVEN BY

GIFT RECEIVED						GIVEN BY

_____			_____

_____			_____

_____			_____

_____			_____

_____			_____

_____			_____

_____			_____

_____			_____

_____			_____

_____			_____

GIFT RECEIVED   GIVEN BY

Made in United States
North Haven, CT
13 March 2023